David Gatward

Leap into Lent

A rundown
through Lent
for teenagers

kevin
mayhew

First published in 2002 by
KEVIN MAYHEW LTD
Buxhall, Stowmarket,
Suffolk, IP14 3BW
E-mail: info@kevinmayhewltd.com

9 8 7 6 5 4 3 2 1 0

ISBN 1 84003 989 2
Catalogue No. 1500550

Cover design by Matt Lockwood
Edited and typeset by Elisabeth Bates
Printed and bound in Great Britain

Contents

Foreword

Lent... right, the official viewpoint is that Lent is all about giving up something you rather like, such as chocolate, a favourite television programme, jam, buying shoes, dancing rather badly, chatting up the opposite sex. It begins with eating lots of pancakes drenched in honey and lemon, and ends at Eastertime when everyone eats lots of expensive chocolate eggs while watching repeat films on a wet Sunday afternoon.

Hang on, that doesn't sound quite right. Let's start again.

First, a brief bit of history. Lent started way, way back in the very earliest days of the Church. It was seen as a time of preparation for Easter. Christians would think about their faith and rededicate themselves to God. Those new to Christianity would be taught all about what it meant to be a Christian and would prepare for baptism.

Lent is the 40-day period before Easter. Because Sunday is seen as the day of the Resurrection, Sundays aren't counted in the 40 days. So, in the Western Church, Lent begins on Ash Wednesday, the seventh Wednesday before Easter.

Easy biblical question: Where else do you hear of 40 days in the Bible?

Easy answer: When Jesus walks off into the wilderness.

By observing the 40 days of Lent, we as individuals can in some way imitate Jesus' own withdrawal into the wilderness for 40 days. A time when he examined what he was about, prayed about his mission, faced up to temptation, and came out the other side with a true understanding of his purpose in this world.

Lent is about taking a look at who you are, what you're about and where you're going to. It's about looking in a mirror and trying to see if the reflection isn't just yours, but God's too. It's a time for saying sorry for the not-so-great stuff in your life and working out ways of sorting things out. It's also an adventure through yourself. Just grab a Bible, chat to God, and travel through all that you are, examining everything about yourself, about you in this world, about where your place here on earth really is. Doesn't that sound like the kind of journey we should all take now and again?

How to use this book

OK, so Lent is about you, about reflection, about reassessing what your life's about. But sometimes, doing that on your own isn't that easy. Which is why this book isn't just for you on your own. Everyone needs guidance, help, advice, and that comes from family, friends, mates. You can use this book on your own or with someone else or a whole group. It isn't full of lengthy passages and hard-to-understand Biblical texts and essays. Instead, it is simply there to get you thinking, to help you ask questions about yourself, your life, your friends, and where Jesus is in it all. And to make it all that much easier, there are four parts to each day.

Bible reading – these are readings selected to help you think through what Lent is all about. To help you understand not just what Jesus was about, but also the background of what was going on, the history and the prophecies, the Bible readings are from both the Old and the New Testament.

Prayer – nothing big or fancy and pages and pages long. Simply a quick prayer to help you focus on your day and get Jesus into the centre of it.

Questions/Activities – This is either something to think about or something to do, or perhaps both! Questions should never be things which weigh us down. Instead, they should help us look at things in a new way, pushing us to discover more about what we are, about this world, about God.

Thought – a quick look at what the Bible readings might be getting at. Something to make you think, to make you talk, to make you quiet, confused, happy, shocked, thoughtful . . .

But what about Sundays? Well, as Sundays aren't included in the 40-day period of Lent, I'm leaving those days free. Sunday is a day of rest, and sometimes that can include a rest from reading stuff that keeps forcing you to think! Use these days as a chance to just let your brain rest from what you've been looking at, what you've been thinking, and get yourself recharged for the week ahead.

A final thought – don't see this book as a set programme for Lent. It is simply a way of getting you thinking about Jesus' life through the 40 days of Lent. You can read it whenever you want with whoever you want. Miss bits out, read bits again, read it alone or with friends. Read around the Bible passages I've used and get a wider, clearer picture of what was going on. This book is just a way of getting you thinking so it's up to you to take it that bit further. Whatever you do, use it to get your brain buzzing about your own life in this world and what Jesus' life, his mission, means to what you're doing with it.

Day 1
Ash Wednesday

Isaiah 58:6-7
I'll tell you what it really means to worship the Lord.
Remove the chains of prisoners who are chained unjustly.
Free those who are abused! Share your food with everyone who is hungry; share your home with the poor and
homeless. Give clothes to those in need; don't turn away
your relatives.

Lord,
    I'm not much good at giving things up.
It seems like a great idea,
    then a few days, hours or minutes later,
    I've started again.

But this time
    I really want to make it count.
I want to give something up
    and learn from the process
    of not giving in to temptation.

I want to wake up
    on day 40 of Lent
    and look in the mirror
    and feel that I've actually achieved something,
    even though it may seem so small.

But by achieving something small
   perhaps it'll lead to bigger
   and better things?
If I can do this,
   then what else can I do?
What else am I capable of?

Help me discover my own potential, Lord.

Amen.

Why is it that pretty much everyone finds it really difficult to give something up?

Write a list of all the things you could give up right now that would actually make your life just that little bit better. Now choose one of those things, write it on a big piece of paper, screw it up, and throw it in the bin. This is what you have given up for Lent – think you can do it?

So, how's that for a Bible reading with punch? Sometimes, it's easy to see the Bible as dull and irrelevant, especially when you find yourself just getting on with everyday life, rushing from here to there, doing this, doing that, paying for this, in debt for that. Then, out of the blue, the Bible metaphorically smacks you good and hard across the face. There you are, in your own little world, when out of the blue you're rubbing a sore cheek and hearing the Bible shouting at you.

'Listen!' it screams at you. 'How obvious do you really need me to be? What else is there I can say? I can't put this any more simply. Wake up!'

So you read it again, get slapped again, and realise that perhaps the Bible isn't that dull or irrelevant after all.

This is a battle cry, though one that doesn't involve politicians, big guns and machoism. Instead, this is a battle cry for justice for all. It's a freedom yell, which echoes through history. It's calling not for us to simply stop doing something, but instead to actually get active, get involved, help the world. Any questions?

Day 2
Time for a change

Psalm 51:1-3, 10
You are kind, God! Please have pity on me. You are always merciful! Please wipe away my sins. Wash me clean from all of my sin and guilt . . . I know about my sins, and I cannot forget my terrible guilt. Create pure thoughts in me and make me faithful again.

Lord,
   it's just dawned on me -
   there's no way I can change,
   no way I can move on in life,
   do something,
   achieve something,
   without first accepting who and what I am
   and what I've done.

I'm not perfect, Lord,
   far from it.
Neither of us need reminding
   of the things I've done wrong.

I want to learn from my mistakes though, Lord,
   and the only way to do that
   is to never make the same mistakes again,
   and to ask for your forgiveness
   for them in the first place.

I'm human and full of faults.
I've got problems and secrets
    and stuff only you and I know about.
But still I sit here, Lord,
    and ask you to be with me,
    to clean me,
    and to walk by my side
    as I step forward into a new day
    and a new me.

Amen.

Is it possible to move on in life without changing anything about yourself?

If you want to progress, what is it about yourself you have to change, say sorry for, accept and move on from?

Have you given something up for Lent that actually used to cost you money? Why not save the money instead? Then, when Lent is over, do something really good with that money you've saved. Why not get some mates to do the same?

Day two and no punches have been pulled. First of all, we see that there's more to fasting than just giving up chocolate. That it's actually got a lot to do with freedom and justice as well. And now we find out that to get anywhere, we have to really see ourselves for what we are.

So, who are you? What are you really like? What secrets do you have? Anything you think God doesn't know about? Who are you kidding! God knows everything about us! God also knows that the only way for us to ever become something more than we already are, to become the person only God knows we can be, is to face up to who we are, accept forgiveness, and then really move on.

Accepting forgiveness isn't easy. It's only possible if you can look yourself in the eye, see everything that you've done, accept what was wrong, and say sorry and really mean it. But there's more to it than that. It's pretty easy to always carry a little bit of baggage, a few things that we just can't forget, that upset us when we think of them. In some ways, we can even use them as scars to be proud of. But that's not right. If we are to accept forgiveness and move on, then we have to get rid of this baggage, throw it away. So ask yourself this – what have you got hidden away that needs putting out with the rubbish?

Day 3
Accepting forgiveness

2 Corinthians 5:20-6:2
We were sent to speak for Christ, and God is begging you to listen to our message. We speak for Christ and sincerely ask you to make peace with God. Christ never sinned! But God treated him as a sinner, so that Christ could make us acceptable to God. We work together with God, and we beg you to make good use of God's kindness to you. In the Scriptures God says, 'When the time came, I listened to you, and when you needed help, I came to save you.' That time has come. This is the day for you to be saved.

Lord,
    accepting forgiveness isn't easy.
Seems daft saying that,
    but it's true.
It's hard enough to look at what I've done,
    the not-so-good stuff in my life,
    and admit all of it in front of you.
It's even harder to believe
    or begin to understand
    that you forgive
    and forget.

A clean slate is frightening, Lord.
No marks, no blemishes,

no dust or chalk marks of old memories.
It's just there,
    for me to do something with,
    a gift from you.

In some ways,
    I don't know what to do with it.
In other ways,
    I'm so excited about what I can really achieve!

This is my new slate, Lord.
A gift from you.
Help me, my Teacher,
    to write a story to be proud of.

Amen.

Are there things in your life you can't really believe you'll ever be forgiven for? Ever wondered why you still bring them up, still remember them? Isn't it about time you moved on, forgot them, got on with your life?

The trouble with giving something up is that it always seems so negative. So why not look at it a different way? OK, so you've given something up, but why not also start something new? Think of something you'd like to learn, or achieve or get better at, or have another go at. Use the next 40 days to see how far you can get with something new.

The whole idea of Jesus, of who and what he was and is, is difficult to grasp. Actually, it's fairly impossible. Think of it for a minute. Jesus, if you believe in him, is the Son of God, born of virgin birth, miracle maker, storyteller, carpenter, friend, brother, son, teacher, servant, visionary, missionary, healer. And that's just for starters. Is it possible that a man such as this could be born into this world to save us from ourselves, from what we were becoming?

Well, here in Paul's second letter to the Corinthians, it's more than a little obvious that he's more than certain as to who Jesus was, what he was about, and what we have to do. It's almost as if he's tripping over his words to get us to hear them. All we have to do is accept that God wants us as friends, not enemies; that we can work with God and achieve amazing things, and that in the end there's just no point in hanging around.

You want to make a difference? You want to really do something? What are you waiting for! Get on with it! Today is the very day to start it!

Day 4
The biggest buzz

Matthew 6:1-6

When you do good deeds don't try to show off. If you do, you won't get a reward from your Father in heaven. When you give to the poor, don't blow a loud horn. That's what show-offs do in the meeting places and on the street corners, because they are always looking for praise. I can assure you that they already have their reward. When you give to the poor, don't let anyone know about it. Then your gift will be given in secret. Your Father knows what is done in secret, and he will reward you. When you pray, don't be like those show-offs who love to stand up and pray in the meeting places and on the street corners. They do this just to look good. I can assure you that they already have their reward. When you pray, go into a room alone and close the door. Pray to your Father in private. He knows what is done in private, and he will reward you.

OK, Lord,
  so I've got this far.
I've accepted I need to change,
  I've asked for forgiveness,
  I've decided to change things about my life,
  and now I hear that you don't really want me
  to make a big deal out of it.

But it is a big deal!
Well, to me, anyway.
These are big changes, Lord,
    this is big stuff that I'm doing.
I want it to get noticed!
I want other people to see it and say,
    'Well done you!'

That's not right though, is it?
After all, what does it matter to others what I do?
What do I gain from boasting a bit?
Not much, I guess.

These are important changes in me, Lord.
Changes I want you to know about
    and others to notice.
Not so my head gets bigger
    but so they ask themselves the question,
    'There's something different, a change –
    I wonder what caused it?'
And if I'm getting people to ask that question,
    then perhaps I'm doing more than I ever imagined?

Amen.

What gives you the biggest buzz – doing something 'good',
or knowing that someone has seen you do it? Why?

Think of something good you can do or get involved with,
find out about it and take part. It can be anything, from

helping someone out to giving money to charity. Now keep this between you and God. It's not a secret, it's simply something you're doing that you don't need to brag about – that's the difference.

First of all, skip back a few pages and you'll find that this passage is just one of many parts of Jesus' Sermon on the Mount. Sitting on a hillside, surrounded by followers and by his disciples, Jesus makes it all rather clear as to how people should live. And this isn't just a bunch of rules meant to be obeyed. These are ideas and thoughts meant to transform lives.

In Matthew 6, Jesus talks about giving, praying and fasting. Jesus isn't big on people showing off about what they do, and here it's made pretty clear as to what's actually important. It's not who sees you do it but what you do that's vital to a good and meaningful life. Nothing we do should be only so that we get praised for doing it. We shouldn't be out to impress by our good deeds. If we are, then are the deeds really all that good? God's not just interested in what we do, but why we do it. Think about it – would you rather someone helped you because they knew you needed help and simply wanted to give you a hand, or because they weren't that bothered about you at all but knew others would look at them and think they were great because of what they were doing? Easy answer, isn't it?

Day 5
Forty days

Luke 4:1-2
When Jesus returned from the River Jordan, the power of
the Holy Spirit was with him, and the Spirit led him into
the desert. For forty days Jesus was tested by the devil,
and during that time he went without eating. When it was
all over, he was hungry.

Lord,
    suddenly 40 days seems like such a long time.
I'm five days in
    and already I'm beginning to wonder
    if I'll make it out the other end.

It's not as though my life's
    radically changed
    and I'm pushing myself to the limit.
All I've really done
    is to decide to give something up,
    have a look at getting involved
    in something else I can learn from,
    and read the Bible and pray regularly.
None of this is big.
None of this is life-changing . . .

Or is it?
Perhaps these are the first small steps

to a better me?
Perhaps all I'm really doing, Lord,
    is learning to walk,
    before learning to run?

Hold my hand, Lord.
    and don't let me fall.
Amen.

Beginning to wonder if you can make it to 40 days? What's stopping you? What are the doubts you've got? Are they really all that important?

How many times have you decided to do something and then given up? How do you feel when you set out on something new and exciting, only to give up later on? What's stopping you from really doing something amazing? How can you change that?

Life gets in the way. It seems to happily fill itself up with loads of stuff to keep you busy, keep your mind racing. It makes sure you haven't got time to stop and think and actually look at the path you're walking. So we end up concentrating on what's immediately in front of us rather than looking ahead. A quote from a film goes something along the lines of, 'You can see the corner, but you're too busy to think about what the road might be like further on.'

Jesus took time out. Not just here, but throughout the small bit of his life we know about. He'd often go and pray and think alone. Why? Because it's important. We sometimes need to step back, think about where we've come from, where we're at, and where we're going to. Lent provides us with the opportunity to do that for a set period of time each year. It makes us forget the excuses for rushing around all the time, and forces us to take our eyes off the corner in the road immediately in front of us and to look at the road further ahead. It's only by doing so that we can ever really have any chance of planning our journey and getting to where we want to be.

Day 6
Freedom

Genesis 3:1-4
The snake was more cunning than any of the other wild animals that the Lord God had made. One day it came to the woman and asked, 'Did God tell you not to eat fruit from any tree in the garden?'

The woman answered, 'God said we could eat fruit from any tree in the garden, except the one in the middle. He told us not to eat fruit from that tree or even to touch it. If we do, we will die.'

'No, you won't!' the snake replied.

Lord,
    freedom's a weird thing.
It's a great gift,
    and also a bit of a pain.
If I wasn't free to choose,
    if I didn't have to make up my own mind
    on what to do with my life,
    everything would be a whole lot easier.
No mistakes would be made,
    no wrong paths taken.
How easy life would be.

But you've given us all that freedom to choose.
It is up to us

to see the right and the wrong
and to make our own decisions.

It was risky, Lord,
     giving us this freedom.
We've run from you,
     ignored you,
     insulted you,
     forgotten you.
But some of us keep coming back.

I'm one of them, Lord -
     help me not to wander too far from home.

Amen.

What does freedom mean to you? What does it mean to other people?

If you had no freedom at all, how would your life be different? What things would you not be able to do?

People all over the world suffer from injustice. They have their freedom stripped from them. They're imprisoned for their beliefs, their words, their actions. But still people fight for freedom. Find out about some of these people, about their lives, about why they thought freedom to be so important.

If you've got time, grab a Bible and have a read through the rest of Genesis 3. It should only take you a couple of minutes. Here we read an explanation of how the bad stuff came into the world, and it's made very clear that it wasn't because God put it there. So where did it come from? Well, it doesn't say, but it does tell us that God gave us the freedom to choose.

Ever wondered why God did this? After all, think of the risk in doing that. If we'd just been left without any freedom, we'd have all believed, all followed, all listened. There would have been no questions . . . and no answers. Without freedom we would never truly be able to achieve, to wonder, to imagine, or to enter into relationship with God. But by being free, we are free to choose either right or wrong. This is the risk God took and perhaps it backfired. Or did it? God wants us to have a relationship with him, and the only way this is possible is for both sides to be fully aware of the consequences. A relationship built without freedom is no relationship at all. God doesn't want us to be with him because we have no choice. Instead, he wants us to be with him because we want to be with him. Makes sense, doesn't it?

Day 7
The risk

Psalm 32:3-5, 8-9
Before I confessed my sins, my bones felt limp, and I groaned all day long. Night and day your hand weighed heavily on me, and my strength was gone as in the summer heat. So I confessed my sins and told them all to you. I said, 'I'll tell the Lord each one of my sins.' Then you forgave me and took away my guilt. . .

You said to me, 'I will point out the road that you should follow. I will be your teacher and watch over you. Don't be stupid like horses and mules that must be led with ropes to make them obey.'

I'm free to choose, Lord.
I can go this way
    or that way.
I can do this or that
    or the other.
It's down to me.

Seems, though,
    that when I go it alone
    I make all the wrong decisions.
I'm 'free to choose', yes,
    but somehow I replace that with
    'free to ignore all your advice'.

So I do things wrong
   and then I come back to you
   and try again.
Not everything goes right.
If it did, what would I ever learn?
But I do know
   that if I try every day
   to keep my eye on you,
   no matter what I do
   I'll always edge that little bit closer
   to the person you want me to be.

Amen.

Why do we abuse our freedom? Why is it that the things we know are wrong seem to be so attractive?

Think of all those things you do wrong that you know you shouldn't, but keep doing anyway. What is it that makes you do them? What's it going to take for you to stop, to walk away and start afresh?

The risk of freedom gives us all the chance to do either the right thing or the wrong thing. And guess which one we seem to be happier to have a go at! We know what's right, we know why it's right. We know what's wrong, we know why it's wrong. But every day we seem to stop, to wander from the path and have a nosey around at what we know is pretty stupid or dangerous.

Read verses 8-9 again. Brilliant aren't they? How clearly do we need it said that God wants to help us, not bind us? He doesn't want us to be stupid like a horse or a mule – how blunt is that? If we don't understand after those words what God wants from us, then we really are lost. God doesn't want to control us. Instead he wants us to live free lives, lives he is actively involved in, excited about, amazed by. This is not a controlling God. This is a God who gives us the gift of freedom, who wants to help us become something amazing, who forgives when we do things wrong and helps us to get back on our feet.

Day 8
New life

Romans 5:18-19
Everyone was going to be punished because Adam sinned. But because of the good thing that Christ has done, God accepts us and gives us the gift of life. Adam disobeyed God and caused many others to be sinners. But Jesus obeyed him and will make many people acceptable to God.

I'm forgiven
   for all the wrong things I do . . .
I wonder how long it'll be
   before I really understand
   what those words mean.

You forgive me,
   you love me.
It's amazing.
It's shocking.
It's real.

I sit here stunned, Lord.
I sit here knowing
   of the wrong I've done
   and that you forgive me for it
   and love me through it.

How can I do anything else
but want to listen to you
and follow you?

Guide me, Lord.

Amen.

What does it mean to you to know that you are forgiven
for all the wrong in your life?

Does being forgiven mean you can just keep doing wrong
and saying sorry?

Think of the times when you've had to say sorry. Was it
just a word or did you have to actually do something to be
truly sorry?

Here, in chapter 5 of Paul's letter to the Romans, we read
about how Jesus' death and resurrection gives us new
life. It's as if our lives, the ups and downs we go through,
now have meaning. Paul compares the sin of Adam and
how we have all been stained by that sin, how it spread
through each and every part of our society, with Jesus
setting us free from it. One man's sin is now completely
and totally outweighed by one man's act.

So this is what we need to get into our thick heads –
that we have sinned, that we are forgiven, that we are set

free. With this freedom we can live lives with God, lives of wonder, of amazement. Lives we can be proud of. Lives we can present to God and say, 'Look! Look what I've done! I've used your gift to the best of my abilities! Look!' In other words, it's time to really start living!

Day 9
A life lived differently

1 Peter 3:8-12
Finally, all of you should agree and have concern and love for each other. You should also be kind and humble. Don't be hateful and insult people just because they are hateful and insult you. Instead, treat everyone with kindness. You are God's chosen ones, and he will bless you. The Scriptures say, 'Do you really love life? Do you want to be happy? Then stop saying cruel things and stop telling lies. Give up your evil ways and do right, as you find and follow the road that leads to peace. The Lord watches over everyone who obeys him, and he listens to their prayers. But he opposes everyone who does evil.'

Lord,
  I want my life to be different.
I don't want to be like everyone else.
I don't want to do the things
    I used to do
    or say the things I used to say.

I want my life to shine.
I want people to see me,
    to know me,
    and to think,
    'Hang on! Something's different here!
    I wonder what it is.'

And I want that 'something different'
     to be you shining through me.

Light me, Lord.

Amen.

How can you really live a life that's different? How can you make your life get people to ask questions?

If we believe in Jesus and follow him, we have to live differently from how we used to. What changes do you need to make?

So we've accepted forgiveness, now what? What are we going to do? Do we just continue as we once were? Do we keep living the same old lives? Do we say the same things, do the same things, act the same way?

Accepting forgiveness involves more than 'sorry'. It means taking those steps forward into a new life, a new you. It means starting again, doing things differently, living a completely new life. This isn't easy and we make mistakes. No one can change over night. But with Jesus, we now have a guide. Someone to take us from where we were, into something completely new and totally exciting. Now we are free to live a life of real worth, a life that each and every day presents us with new challenges, new adventures, new experiences, and all in the presence of God. Just how amazing does that sound?

Day 10
Temptation

Matthew 4:1-4

The Holy Spirit led Jesus into the desert, so that the devil could test him. After Jesus had gone without eating for forty days and nights, he was very hungry. Then the devil came to him and said, 'If you are God's Son, tell these stones to turn into bread.'

Jesus answered, 'The Scriptures say, "No one can live only on food. People need every word that God has spoken."'

OK, Lord,
    I've made up my mind
    and want to live a life
    that I can give to you
    as a gift.
A life that has you
    shining through it.

But something's worrying me.
I'm weak, Lord.
I'm just a human,
    with human worries,
    and human weaknesses.
I'm afraid I'll fall, Lord,
    that after all these good intentions,
    I'll still make a mess of it
    and give up.

Help me, Lord,
    to not give in.
Temptation isn't something I have to give in to
    or to be afraid of,
    not if I'm with you all the way.

Keep me safe, Lord.

Amen.

What things do you know trip you up, no matter what you do? Why is it so easy to give in?

Next time you find yourself falling away from God, giving in to something that you know isn't right, what are you going to do?

Here, Jesus faces up to the things which will test him as he begins his ministry. He has power and it is down to him how he uses it. He can use it for his own purposes, or for God's. That's why Jesus experiences these tests out in the desert. He's hungry, so why not just turn the stone to bread? Pretty easy stuff if you're the Son of God. Read further on and you'll find the other temptations. Why not test God? Tell you what, why not jump off a huge building and have angels save you?

Each time, Jesus answers with a quote from Scripture, and the first one is rather important. We seem to think we have everything we need because we only think about what we can touch, feel, taste, see. But wait a minute! What's the slight empty feeling inside? And what about that odd feeling that there must be more to life than this? That there must be a purpose? You can't live on just what's around you. Well you can, but it's a bit of an empty existence. There's more to life than that, and you only find that out by grasping tight the outstretched hand of God.

Day 11
Do not be afraid

Genesis 15:1-6

Later the Lord spoke to Abram in a vision, 'Abram, don't be afraid! I will protect you and reward you greatly.'

But Abram answered, 'Lord All-Powerful, you have given me everything I could ask for, except children. And when I die, Eliezer of Damascus will get all I own. You have not given me any children and this servant of mine will inherit everything.'

The Lord replied, 'No, he won't! You will have a son of your own, and everything you have will be his.' Then the Lord took Abram outside and said, 'Look at the sky and see if you can count the stars. That's how many descendants you will have.'

Where to now, Lord?
What do I do?
What next?
What effect will you have on my life?
Will I change?
Where will I see your influence
    in my everyday life?
Will I hear your voice?
Will I see you at work?
Will I understand you
    and do as you ask?

Will my faith be strong?
Will I fall away from you?
Will I stand strong?
What will be my reward?

Be the answer to all my questions, Lord.

Amen.

What questions do you have that you really want answered? About you, about your life, about today and tomorrow and for ever?

What kind of effect do you want God to have on your life? Are you going to let doubt stand in the way?

Abram, which means 'exalted father', is very soon to become Abraham, which means 'father of many'. This man who has true faith in God, is to become the father of nations. But, like any of us, he's not completely convinced or sure. How can he become the father of so many if he can't even produce an heir? He, like any of us, when presented with what God's actually about, has doubts.

Then we're given a wonderful picture. 'Look at the sky and try to count the stars . . .' How's that for an image! God is making it pretty obvious right there and then that indeed Abram will be the father of nations. So what about you? What do you think God wants to do with your life?

Abram was just a man, but he had faith. You are no different and God loves you just as much, that same God that spoke to Abram. For a moment, just try to imagine all that you are capable of, all that you can do, all that could happen in just your life. Amazed yet? Now look at the stars and just think about that promise to Abram all those years ago.

Day 12
God's love

Psalm 27:1-6

You, Lord, are the light that keeps me safe. I am not afraid of anyone. You protect me, and I have no fears. Brutal people may attack and try to kill me, but they will stumble. Fierce enemies may attack, but they will fall. Armies may surround me, but I won't be afraid; war may break out, but I will trust you. I ask only one thing, Lord: Let me live in your house every day of my life to see how wonderful you are and to pray in your temple. In times of trouble, you will protect me. You will hide me in your tent and keep me safe on top of a mighty rock. You will let me defeat all of my enemies. Then I will celebrate, as I enter your tent with animal sacrifices and songs of praise.

Lord,
    knowing you love me,
    that you want to get to know me,
    is quite a weird thought.
My Creator,
    someone so powerful,
    wanting to chat to me,
    listen to me,
    cry with me,
    walk with me.

Is this for real?
Have you thought this through?
I mean I'm not all that great really.
I'm a bit of a nobody,
    a face in a crowd.

But the evidence speaks for itself.
I read passages like this
    and can't help but feel that bit more secure,
    that bit more safe.
As though my life now has purpose,
    has meaning.

Thank you, Lord.

Amen.

What does God's love mean to you? How does it make you feel?

How does God's love for you affect the way you treat other people?

A relationship with God is in many ways very different from any other relationship you may have. But in many ways, it is also very similar. It's a two-way thing. It only works if both sides want to make it work. That means you have to work at it and so does God. It also means that if you believe and trust, then the rewards are huge.

Take a look at this passage again, and if you've got a Bible nearby, read the rest of the psalm. God protects us, saves us, shelters us. That's quite something really, isn't it? But what does this really mean? Does it mean that believing in God makes life nice and easy, with nothing going wrong, nothing bad happening, no one getting hurt? Er, no, sorry. What it does mean though, is that we are not alone in our lives any more. Think of the way your friendships with people help protect you from life's mishaps. How when you're down, they help you out, cheer you up. God does this and more. Protection doesn't just mean a big wall to hide behind, it means giving you the capability to face life head on and make something of it, no matter what it may throw at you.

Day 13
God's promise

Romans 4:20-25
But Abraham never doubted or questioned God's promise. His faith made him strong, and he gave all the credit to God. Abraham was certain that God could do what he had promised. So God accepted him, just as we read in the Scriptures. But these words were not written only for Abraham. They were written for us, since we will also be accepted because of our faith in God, who raised our Lord Jesus to life. God gave Jesus to die for our sins, and he raised him to life, so that we would be made acceptable to God.

Faith's difficult, Lord.
Life puts up so many obstacles
    that most of the time
    I can hardly see you.

At times like this, Lord,
    you seem so far away.
I sometimes feel that I'm fooling myself,
    that you don't exist,
    that I'm wasting my time.

But I keep thinking back to your life
    here on earth.

No matter how many doubts I have,
   you seem to be able to make me sit up
   and listen.
A life lived so long ago
   affecting a life lived right here and now.

It seems amazing, Lord,
   and if all those things you did and said
   are true,
   then I have no option
   but to believe
   and follow.

Never let me leave you, Lord.

Amen.

God's promised you – that person you see in the mirror every day – eternal life. That's quite a promise. Do you doubt this promise, or do you hold on to it, excited about what it really means?

Promises. Well, we all make them, we all keep them, we all break them. But this is something different. When God makes a promise, then there's no going back on it. So that's not where the problem lies. Instead, it lies with us. We find it so hard to believe the promises of God, that we doubt, we ignore what God shows us through the life of Jesus.

You'd think that eventually God would get tired of everyone doubting, and just give up. Not so, though. Instead, the promise stays and he forgives and he rejoices every time someone new accepts him, every time someone accepts his forgiveness; every time you turn back to God and get on the right track again. God's promise is exactly that – a promise. It's not for the breaking.

Day 14
Jesus speaks about his death

Mark 8:31-33

Jesus began telling his disciples what would happen to him. He said, 'The nation's leaders, the chief priests, and the teachers of the Law of Moses will make the Son of Man suffer terribly. He will be rejected and killed, but three days later he will rise to life.'

Then Jesus explained clearly what he meant. Peter took Jesus aside and told him to stop talking like that. But when Jesus turned and saw the disciples, he corrected Peter. He said to him, 'Satan, get away from me! You are thinking like everyone else and not like God.'

It's no wonder
    they didn't quite understand, Lord.
There you were,
    their teacher,
    their leader,
    their inspiration.
Then out of the blue
    you start to tell them
    that you were to die
    and then rise again.

At what point would any of that make sense
    to anyone?

Most of the time
  it doesn't make any sense to me.
I respond a bit like Peter,
  all shouts and confusion,
  or just sit quiet,
  not knowing quite what to make of it.

Help me to understand, Lord.

Amen.

If you'd been there, with Jesus, and heard him talk about his death, how would you have reacted? What would you have thought?

If you skim back through the pages of Mark you'll notice that this is quite a moment. For the first time we have Jesus telling his disciples that he will suffer death, and then rise again. This is front-page news, earthquake news, news that topples mountains. It's not really surprising that the disciples don't quite get it. Would you?

Peter rebukes Jesus. We may not be given his words, but you can easily imagine the response Peter gave after this news from Jesus. 'What are you talking about? That's rubbish! Death? What's that got to do with you teaching us and leading us? Are you mad?' Peter seems to fill that all-too-human role so easily, and in many ways helps us all see how we would perhaps react in the same situation, or, indeed any situation where Jesus challenges us. We open our mouths, we close our minds, and we shout. What we need to do is stop, think, and to try and understand.

Day 15
Losing life to save it

Mark 8:34-38

Jesus then told the crowd and the disciples to come closer, and he said: 'If any of you want to be my followers, you must forget about yourself. You must take up your cross and follow me. If you want to save your life, you will destroy it. But if you give up your life for me and for the good news, you will save it. What will you gain, if you own the whole world but destroy yourself? What could you give to get back your soul? Don't be ashamed of me and my message among these unfaithful and sinful people! If you are, the Son of Man will be ashamed of you when he comes in the glory of his Father with the holy angels.

So this is what is required of me, Lord.
Seems quite a tall order, really.
Losing my life for you
    so that I can save it?
Where's the sense in that?
Seems a bit of a waste.

Though it does make sense as well,
    I guess.
It can be easy to become obsessed
    with the trimmings of life,

the sparkly bits,
the money,
the sugar coating.
But what you're asking
is for us to forget that
and to actually do something worthwhile
with this life-gift.
To live it not for ourselves
but for others,
for you.
To be so happy with the gift
that all we want to do
is use it to benefit others
rather than ourselves.
That to me, Lord,
sounds a lot more exciting
than just living for myself.

Help me live my life to the full, Lord.

Amen.

What do you really want to do with your life? What do you want to achieve?

It's easy to become self-obsessed, and sometimes it's not even your fault. The world pushes you into a corner, forces you to keep your head down as you try to achieve, achieve, achieve. Soon you believe that what's really important is wealth, power, prosperity. But what are these thoughts pushing out? What are they stopping you from becoming, from achieving?

So Jesus has mentioned for the first time his death and resurrection. He's had a bit of a run in with Peter and now he's turned to the crowd. It's time for them to understand exactly what life is about, what is required of those who hear him, who follow him.

His words are initially frightening. Forgetting self and carrying a cross? Losing life to save it? Where's the sense in any of it? It seems that as well as presenting messages through stories and parables, sometimes Jesus wanted to get straight to the point, shock tactics. But what do his words mean to us, here and now? Easy – Jesus wants commitment. He doesn't want us to just say, 'Yeah, man, like Jesus is sooooo coooooool!' and then just go on living as normal. Instead, he wants us to hear him, understand him, and follow his lead. Jesus was a single candle, burning like crazy in the darkness. He in turn wants us to be candles, to burn fiercely. And the only way to do that is to want to burn, to give it our all.

And what would you rather be anyway; a damp firework that goes 'fztzzz' and dies, or a huge candle that in even the wildest of storms, keeps burning?

Day 16
God so loved the world

John 3:16-17
God loved the people of this world so much that he gave his only Son, so that everyone who has faith in him will have eternal life and never really die. God did not send his Son into the world to condemn its people. He sent him to save them!

Eternal life, Lord.
What's it like?
It seems an idiotic thing to be talking about.
It's impossible, surely?
How can I live for ever?
And what do you do with all that time
    if you are living for ever?

I think like this because I don't understand,
    because I'm used to a life based on the 24-hour day.
A life where the sun wakes me
    and the moon closes my eyes.
A life where I get older,
    where years run by quicker
    and death is guaranteed.
But this talk of eternal life,
    of more beyond what I'm doing here and now,
    gives me hope.

Living for ever, Lord?
Really?
You promise?

Amen.

What do you think eternal life will be like? How will it be different from our life here on earth?

Jesus didn't want us to think only of the reward of following him. We are not to rush through life, thinking it to be a bit rubbish, so that we can get to heaven more quickly. We are here to live life to the full. How are you going to do that?

This is possibly one of the most famous bits of John's Gospel; 'God loved the people of this world so much that he gave his only Son, so that everyone who has faith in him will have eternal life.'

Death is a scary thing. It's an unnerving but simple truth that everyone dies eventually. But Jesus stares us in the face with his life. He grabs our attention, looks us in the eye and says, 'Look! What are you afraid of? Death just hasn't got a hold any more! Look at what I've shown you. Follow me. Come on – I promise you, eternal life is yours and it's better than you could ever imagine!' No one knows what death is like until they've done it. No one that is, except Jesus. And if we believe in him, we can live every day bursting with hope. Death? Bring it on – we're not afraid any more!

Day 17
A great life

Isaiah 55:1-3

If you are thirsty, come and drink the water! If you don't have any money, come, eat what you want! Drink wine and milk without paying a penny. Why waste your money on what isn't really food? Why work hard for something that doesn't satisfy? Listen carefully to me, and you will enjoy the very best foods. Pay close attention! Come to me and live. I will promise you the eternal love and loyalty that I promised David.

Sometimes, Lord,
   you seem so far away.
Like a fairytale told to me as a child.
But other times,
   you seem so close,
    it's hard to get away!

Occasionally,
   there's a sudden realisation in my brain –
   the thought that above all,
   beyond all hope,
   all you really want to do
   is to help us,
   and love us.
It's that simple!

You're not about making life difficult.
You don't want us to have a bad time.
You want to give us life!

That's quite something, Lord.
The thought that my Creator
   wants to help me live life to the full,
   and is there by my side all the way.
If I follow you,
   how can I help but do something right
   with my life?

Watch me live, Lord.

Amen.

OK, this is how it is: God not only wants you to have a great and amazing life, but actually wants to help you achieve it and do it! How does that make you feel?

Knowing that this is what God's about, how do you think the way you live your life will change? What changes can you make right now, today?

Isaiah 55 is all about God saying to his people, 'Listen! I love you! I always have, I always will! I have so much I want to give you!' And when God says something like that, you can't help but take notice. But God doesn't just say this to some people and not others, these are words for all ears, including yours.

It's easy to forget that God promises to be with us, to help us, to love us. That what he really wants is for us to live brilliantly with him. But reading words like this helps to remind us what's really going on. That's why we should read the Bible as often as we can. God inspired people to write these words, his words, for everyone. How can we ever really know what's going on, if we don't sit down and read about it now and again?

Day 18
This world

Psalm 19:1-6

The heavens keep telling the wonders of God, and the skies declare what he has done. Each day informs the following day; each night announces to the next. They don't speak a word, and there is never the sound of a voice. Yet their message reaches all the earth, and it travels around the world. In the heavens a tent is set up for the sun. It rises like a bridegroom and gets ready like a hero eager to run a race. It travels all the way across the sky. Nothing hides from its heat.

This world, Lord,
   is amazing.
No matter how awful I feel,
   I can still look at this world
   and feel a smile creep across my face.

I've seen so little of it first-hand.
There's so much of it
   I'll probably never ever see.
But the bits I've walked on,
   passed by,
   heard,
   touched,
   tasted,

climbed . . .
astound me.

This world is a gift of such wonder,
that words fail me, Lord.

Amen.

Do you have a favourite place? What do you like about it?
Think about it for a moment, imagine that you're there.
What have you got to say to God about it?

This world is great, but we're not doing much to keep it
that way. What do you do to help make sure we don't ruin
this world for ever?

Whoever wrote this psalm was obviously rather excited.
It's almost as though he'd got up early one day, gone for
a quick walk, and been overcome with one of the most
beautiful mornings he'd ever experienced. The sun was
out, the sky was blue, the air clear. Torn between staying
out in the beauty of the day or going home to write about
it, he quickly runs back as fast as possible to get his
thoughts, his poetry, down on a loose scroll before the
words, the day, the image disappears.

   He begins with, 'The heavens keep telling the wonders
of God, and the skies declare what he has done.' Did he
walk outside and find himself almost yelling these words

out loud? It's as if it is all so utterly obvious to him that he just doesn't want to mess around with clever words and metaphors. 'This is it!' he says to us. 'Just go look outside and you'll see God's glory! Go on! Get out there and see it for yourselves!' So, why don't you?

Day 19
Worth dying for

Romans 5:6-8
Christ died for us at a time when we were helpless and sinful. No one is really willing to die for an honest person, though someone might be willing to die for a truly good person. But God showed how much he loved us by having Christ die for us, even though we were sinful.

I'm not sure I'm up to it, Lord.
I'm not sure
    I can follow you
    in the way you want me to.

Believing in you makes sense.
It gives hope,
    makes life have meaning.
But there's more to it than that.

I know people have died
    because they believed in you,
    followed you.
Since you trod this earth
    people have been killed
    because they refused to go against you.

I'm not sure I'm up to that.
I'm not sure that if I was pushed

I wouldn't just give up.
Even Peter denied knowing you,
    and I'm just little old me.

It scares me, Lord,
    what you require from us.
It frightens me
    that I might not be strong enough,
    that I might fail.

Stand by me, Lord,
    and give me strength.

Amen.

Do you find that sometimes you go against what you believe? Why do you think you do this? What can you do to stop it? Ever asked God for help?

People all over the world have laid down their lives because of their belief not only in Jesus, but in justice and freedom. Why not find out about some of these people and learn from the lives they lead?

How far would you go to save the life of someone you really didn't like? What would you do? Hard to say, isn't it? It's hard enough to think that you would ever have to save or help someone you don't like, but the thought of dying for them? What's that all about, then?

But the paradox of Jesus' life isn't just that he died for everyone, even though we're full to bursting with sin, but that he loves us even though we are sinners! It's not a case of dying for someone he doesn't like. This is about loving us so much that instead of losing us all, he takes our place. The sins of the world? Well, just you watch what one man can do with it.

Day 20
Not giving in

1 Corinthians 10:12-13
Even if you think you can stand up to temptation, be careful not to fall. You are tempted in the same way that everyone else is tempted. But God can be trusted not to let you be tempted too much, and he will show you how to escape from your temptations.

Did you ever think you'd fail, Lord,
   when you knew you were soon to die?
When you knew that in the weeks to follow
   you would be whipped, beaten,
   scorned, broken,
   cast out,
   then nailed to some wood to die?

Did you ever wonder if it was worth it?
Did you ever think you were wrong?
Did you ever feel that you no longer had the strength?

It's a shocking story, Lord.
What you went through, it scares me.
I don't like to read about it.
I don't like to think about it.
I don't enjoy trying to understand it.

But you turned it all on it's head.
You took what seemed to be the end,
    and changed it for ever.
Your death not only tore the curtains in the temple,
    but the hold that sin and death had on your people,
    on me.

Thank you for my freedom, Lord.

Amen.

Are there times in life when you just want to give up? When you feel that you've had enough and can't go on, can't take any more? What is it that keeps you going? What gives you the strength not to give in?

Life is a constant barrage of challenges. Some we can meet, some we're not sure about, some we're afraid of, and some we hope we never have to meet. But it is often through challenges that we discover new things about who and what we are, what we're capable of. By pushing ourselves, by existing in situations that make us feel uncomfortable, we can become so much more than we originally thought.

Imagine if all the challenge in your life was removed. Imagine if it didn't take any effort to do anything, if it was all handed to you on a plate. Think what it would be like to live a life where everything was easy, simple, no worries.

A life where there was no risk of failure, no risk that you would get hurt, no danger. What life would that be? No life at all, at a guess. So which would you rather have?

Day 21
This is my own dear Son

Matthew 17:1-3, 5
Six days later, Jesus took Peter and the brothers James
and John with him. They went up on a very high mountain
where they could be alone. There in front of the disciples,
Jesus was completely changed. His face was shining like
the sun, and his clothes became white as light. All at once
Moses and Elijah were there talking with Jesus. . .

While Peter was still speaking, the shadow of a bright
cloud passed over them. From the cloud a voice said, 'This
is my own dear Son, and I am pleased with him. Listen to
what he says!'

This is a difficult one to understand, Lord.
There you are,
    with your three closest disciples,
    and out of the blue
    you're standing with Moses and Elijah.

What am I supposed to do with this story?
It seems impossible,
    crazy,
    insane.
How could it happen?
How could they know it was Moses and Elijah?
But what if it did happen?

What if this is not just a story
but a reality,
an event in time?

That changes things, Lord.
It makes me look at everything you did,
everything you are,
and really wonder
about what
and who
you are.

Amen.

What would you have done if you were one of the disciples and you'd seen Elijah and Moses with Jesus? How would you have reacted?

Sometimes we all crave to actually hear God's voice. To hear God speaking to us in the same way we hear others speaking to us. Now just think about what it would be like if that did actually happen – the voice of your Creator calling for you, talking to you. How do you think you'd react?

If you've read through the stories about Jesus before this event, it's quite easy to see that the disciples by now were more than certain as to who Jesus was – the Messiah. This event – where they are suddenly witness to Jesus not just being their leader, but something almost beyond comprehension, shining in glory – stops them in their tracks. It reassures them as to who Jesus is, it gives them a glimpse of his glory, his power. If you check out Luke 9:31, you'll read that Elijah and Moses talked with Jesus about his death. And it's from this point on that Jesus begins to talk more and more about his death. Read Matthew 17:9. Here Jesus warns them not to tell anyone about this vision they have seen 'until the Son of Man has been raised from death'. The disciples must have realised at that time, even though they may not have fully understood, that Jesus was talking about himself, his own death, his own resurrection.

Day 22
Jesus in the temple

Matthew 21:12-14
Jesus went into the temple and chased out everyone who was selling or buying. He turned over the tables of the moneychangers and the benches of the ones who were selling doves. He told them, 'The Scriptures say, "My house should be called a place of worship." But you have turned it into a place where robbers hide.' Blind and lame people came to Jesus in the temple and he healed them.

Was there a fire in your eyes, Lord?
Did you not only drive out the moneychangers,
　　but scare them a little as well?
Did any of them dare stand up to you
　　as you burst through them,
　　driving out the animals,
　　tipping over their tables?

I wouldn't mind a bit of that fire myself, Lord.
I'm not saying I want to run wild at church
　　and drive out the choir for singing badly,
　　but there are things in this world,
　　stuff going on,
　　that needs driving out,
　　turning over.

But the same goes for me, Lord.
There are things in my life,
   things I do and say and think –
   and I need you to help me
   drive them out.

Turn over the tables in my life, Lord.

Amen.

How angry does injustice make you feel? Do you feel helpless, desperate to make a difference? What's stopping you
doing something, standing up for what's right, getting
involved?

Jesus has just entered Jerusalem (Matthew 21:1-11) and
everyone's cheering for him, as he rides through the
streets on a colt. Then he goes to the temple. It seems
impossible to read this without imagining Jesus as angry.
What? Jesus, the Son of God, angry? Yes, angry. As he
goes to the temple, perhaps he sees outside the people
who really need to get in there: the blind, the lame, the
poor. They can't get in because the temple is full of people
dealing money, selling animals for sacrifice. Who knows
what else was going on? Words aren't enough and Jesus
goes for them, tipping over the tables, driving out the
animals. Then the blind and the crippled come to him in
the temple and he heals them. By his actions, Jesus brings

about change. He knew that words simply wouldn't have worked. Now look at your life. Are there areas where rather than just talking about it, it's about time you just did something instead?

Day 23
An unlikely choice

1 Samuel 16:10-12

Jesse sent all seven of his sons over to Samuel. Finally, Samuel said, 'Jesse, the Lord hasn't chosen any of these young men. Do you have any more sons?'

'Yes,' Jesse answered. 'My youngest son David is out taking care of the sheep.'

'Send for him!' Samuel said. 'We won't start the ceremony until he gets here.'

Jesse sent for David. He was a healthy, good-looking boy with a sparkle in his eyes. As soon as David came, the Lord told Samuel, 'He's the one! Get up and pour the olive oil on his head.'

Lord,
   you seemed an unlikely choice.
Everyone wanted their version of the Messiah.
They wanted a King to come in glory.
They wanted revolution,
   a Saviour who would lead them
   out of the hands of the Romans
   and into freedom.
They wanted glory
   with all the trimmings.

But you were different.
You turned their ideas on their head.

You came as a quiet King.
You came from a background
   so many of them would understand.
You knew their lives,
   their very hopes and fears.

You came not to save by might and power and glory
   but by teaching,
   and helping,
   and healing,
   and serving.

Amen.

Everyone hoped for a Messiah and they knew what they were looking for. Someone to come in the power of God, his glory blazing, smiting the enemies and bringing them to freedom from oppression. They got something a bit different. It's no wonder that many didn't really understand what Jesus was all about. How do you think you'd have reacted back then? What would you have thought of Jesus?

The story of David is quite amazing, and it's up there with many people's favourite Bible stories. Israel has a king – Saul. He was chosen by God and had done a great job. But something went wrong, Saul turned away from God. So God gets Samuel to find the new king of Israel. Samuel isn't too happy about this. In 1 Samuel 16:2, when told by God that he has chosen a son of someone called Jesse, Samuel says, 'If I do that Saul will find out and have me killed.' But he trusts and does what God wants and heads off to Bethlehem. The first son Samuel meets is Eliab and he's convinced right away that this must be the chosen one. But God says, 'Pay no attention to how tall and hand-some he is. I have rejected him, because I do not judge as people judge. They look at the outward appearance, but I look at the heart.' Samuel then sees all the other sons, until finally the only one left is the youngest, the shepherd boy, the most unlikely of all the brothers to be king. It was unexpected, even for Samuel. It's no wonder that Jesus, unlike anything anyone had expected, upset a few people, is it?

Day 24
The Lord is my shepherd

Psalm 23:1-3, 6

You, Lord, are my shepherd. I will never be in need. You let me rest in fields of green grass. You lead me to streams of peaceful water, and you refresh my life. You are true to your name, and you lead me along the right paths.

Your kindness and love will always be with me each day of my life, and I will live for ever in your house, Lord.

Lord,
    sometimes I feel
    like I need a shepherd.
Someone to guide me,
    to protect me,
    to look after me
    and those around me.

The world outside
    can feel so hostile,
    and I feel so helpless.
The only way to survive it,
    to get through life,
    is with you helping me,
    leading me,
    guiding me.

Watch over me, Lord,
and don't let me wander too far
from the rest of your flock.

Amen.

Life's not easy, but then if it was, would we enjoy it as much? Would we get as much out of it? We all need help and guidance at different times from all types of people. Think of those who have helped you in your life, the impact they've had on you and how you live. Have you ever really thanked God for them?

This is by far the best-known of all the psalms. It is also one of the favourite images of God, the Good Shepherd. Shepherds are amazing. They go out in all weathers to look after their flock. They feed them and protect them. They find shelter for them and heal them. Back in the days of David, and in the days of Jesus, a shepherd's life was also at risk. Protecting your flock meant lying across the front of the fold, the entrance to where the sheep were kept for the night. This way the sheep wouldn't escape and also the shepherd would know if any wolves or bears were coming nearby. If you read verse 5 in your Bible you'll also see how God is the perfect host, welcoming us as honoured guests. This is quite a God! A God who helps us and protects us and leads us and also welcomes us with open arms. A God willing to sacrifice himself for us in order to protect us.

Day 25
Sacrifice

Psalm 107:17-22
Some of you had foolishly committed a lot of sins and were in terrible pain. The very thought of food was disgusting to you, and you were almost dead. You were in serious trouble, but you prayed to the Lord, and he rescued you. By the power of his own word, he healed you and saved you from destruction. You should praise the Lord for his love and for the wonderful things he does for all of us. You should celebrate by offering sacrifices and singing joyful songs to tell what he has done.

Sacrifices, Lord?
How can I thank you like that?
I'm not really keen
    on the whole idea
    of presenting you with an animal
    as a way of saying thanks.
Doesn't seem quite right.
So what can I offer?
How can I say thanks?

My life is nothing, really.
I seem to mess it up so often,
    do stupid things,
    ignore you

and do what I think is right.
What do I have to offer?

Nothing, Lord.
I look at what I have to give you,
    and I can't see anything worth giving.
But that can't be right, can it?
If I am worth nothing,
    why do you love me?
Why do you want me to do something
    with my life?

Maybe that's the sacrifice I can offer?
Everything that I am,
    everything that I do,
    for you?

Amen.

How often do you think about what God's done in your life so far? Do you ever look back and think, 'Yep, God helped me.' And if so, how do you thank him? What sacrifice can you offer to God as a way of thanks, a way of showing exactly how you feel?

In the Old Testament it sometimes seems that people were sacrificing all the time. Get an animal, say thanks to God, kill the animal. Remember though that this was a long, long time ago. An animal was something of huge value to a household. It was their food, their livelihood. It wasn't just something done because it had to be done. It would cost them a great deal. And when trying to thank God, to really show what they felt, the most costly way to do that, to prove they loved him, was to give their most valued gift. And this, more often than not, was an animal. That's what sacrifice is all about. Giving something that means so much to you, that is all that you are, to someone else. That's real sacrifice. Now take that a step further. How much greater the sacrifice when you give your life for someone else's! To turn around and say, 'No! Take me instead! Let this person live, because I love them this much.' That's real sacrifice and something few, if any, can see through to the end.

Day 26
True healing

John 9:1-3a, 6-7
As Jesus walked along, he saw a man who had been blind since birth. Jesus' disciples asked, 'Teacher, why was this man born blind? Was it because he or his parents sinned?'
   'No, it wasn't!' Jesus answered.
After Jesus said this, he spat on the ground. He made some mud and smeared it on the man's eyes. Then he said, 'Go and wash off the mud in Siloam Pool.' The man went and washed in Siloam, which means 'One who is sent'. When he had washed off the mud, he could see.

Lord,
    the power to heal people
    amazes me.
You were brought up as an ordinary man
    from an ordinary place.
You had ordinary friends
    and an ordinary job.
Yet you did extraordinary things.

This man was blind,
    and you healed him.
You did something
    that doesn't fit in with the order of things.
It upsets the way things are,
    the way we accept them to be.

In that moment
   you were outside all the rules,
   all the conventions.
But does that mean you broke them,
   or simply worked perfectly in them?

Your power is something so beyond
   anything I can imagine
   that all I can do
   is take notice.

Amen.

Sometimes it can be easy to think, 'Oh no! This has happened to me because I did that!' But is this really the case? Are we really punished in this way? Or is it that when we do what is wrong, we find ourselves further away from God, from his world, from what we can be? Is the punishment for our sin not something really obvious but instead the knowledge that we've done wrong and the effect that has on us and the world around us?

The disciples ask a simple question: 'Teacher, whose sin has caused him to be born blind?' They believed that there was a connection between sin and suffering and that this could well be people's illness and afflictions. This is why you quite often read about Jesus forgiving people before healing them. They needed to know they were forgiven before they could be healed because only by doing this would they have faith enough to be healed. Here, though, the connection between suffering and sin is made, but it doesn't mean that someone will suffer something such as blindness because of their own or their parents' sin. Basically, sin's a bigger issue – it's a worldwide epidemic rather than something that makes an individual go blind. And out of this man's individual suffering, Jesus brings about something good – he heals him and he can see and also he believes. In the same way out of the wrong in our own lives, Jesus seems to be able to bring about something good so long as we trust him and follow him.

Day 27
The freedom to come back

Luke 15:1-7

Tax collectors and sinners were all crowding around to listen to Jesus. So the Pharisees and the teachers of the Law of Moses started grumbling, 'This man is friendly with sinners. He even eats with them.' Then Jesus told them this story:

If any of you has a hundred sheep, and one of them gets lost, what will you do? Won't you leave the ninety-nine in the field and go and look for the lost sheep until you find it? And when you find it, you will be so glad that you will put it on your shoulder and carry it home. Then you will call in your friends and neighbours and say, 'Let's celebrate! I've found my lost sheep!'

Jesus said, 'In the same way there is more happiness in heaven because of one sinner who turns to God than over ninety-nine good people who don't need to.'

It's hard to believe
  that anyone would be all that happy
  to save me, Lord.
I'm nothing really –
  just a little life
  in a very big world.
The thought that my coming to you,
  saying sorry for what I've done,

accepting who you are
and what you can do for me,
would cause joy in heaven,
seems crazy.

Is it true, Lord?
Are you really that happy
    that I talk to you,
    try to listen to you
    and understand you?
Does it really mean that much to you
    that someone like me
    has decided to try to follow you?
Really?

Amen.

If you lose something really valuable, something that means a lot to you, how do you feel? How does it affect your day? What do you do about it? And how do you feel if you finally find it? What do you do then?

OK, get this: God is amazingly happy when people turn to him, accept him, listen to him, and believe. We're not talking just normal happy, but a happiness which involves tears and laughter and trumpets and knocking on neighbours' doors to tell them! Not only that, God goes to all lengths to get in touch with everyone, to get them back. He never stops caring, never stops loving. This is a God utterly obsessed with his creation, filled with an endless love for them, even though they've ignored him and wandered off. But this is a love so real, so strong, that he doesn't force people to believe, to see him, to come back to him. In his love he gives us all the freedom to come back, so that the relationship is free to grow and develop and become something even more amazing. A God who goes out of his way to throw the biggest celebration ever each time someone comes back.

Day 28
The lost son

Luke 15:11-14
Jesus also told them another story:

Once a man had two sons. The younger son said to his father, 'Give me my share of the property.' So the father divided his property between his two sons. Not long after that, the younger son packed up everything he owned and left for a foreign country, where he wasted all his money in wild living. He had spent everything, when a bad famine spread through that whole land. Soon he had nothing to eat.

I get the impression, Lord,
    that this is exactly what we did.
We, your people,
    were given so much by you.
And instead of making good use of it,
    living with it,
    loving it,
    we took it and wasted it.
All that you gave
    we took for granted,
    spent it,
    and before we knew it,
    there was nothing left.

What choice do we have
    but to come back to you?
We're not worthy of forgiveness,
    not after what we've done.
But it's all we can hope for
    and it is also what you give.

You amaze me, Lord.

Amen.

What things do you think you've wasted? Are there talents you have that you're not using in the way that you could? Are there gifts you know you've been given that you've either used wrongly or just ignored? What are you going to do about it?

If someone wasted something you'd given them, or left you, ignored you, then came back to ask for forgiveness, how would you react?

Although I've only included up to verse 14 here, I reckon the best thing you could now do is to open your Bible and read the rest of the story. You'll probably remember most of it, but refresh your memory. The younger son wastes his father's gift, asks for forgiveness and receives it. The father orders a huge party to take place. The elder son doesn't understand and certainly doesn't think the younger son deserves any of it. But the father tells him to celebrate. Although he has been with his father all along, his brother who was dead is now alive; a lost son has returned. And what do we learn from this? God is like the father, overwhelmed with happiness at the return of a lost son. The elder son is like those who don't quite get it and certainly don't like the idea of God welcoming bad people, dirty people, sinners, to him. But that's what God's about. The past is forgiven, it's a fresh start, and what a celebration it is!

Day 29

A new covenant

Jeremiah 31:31-34

The Lord said, 'The time will surely come when I will make a new agreement with the people of Israel and Judah. It will be different from the agreement I made with their ancestors when I led them out of Egypt. Although I was their God, they broke that agreement. Here is the new agreement that I, the Lord, will make with the people of Israel: "I will write my laws on their hearts and minds. I will be their God and they will be my people." No longer will they have to teach one another to obey me. I, the Lord, promise that all of them will obey me, ordinary people and rulers alike. I will forgive their sins and forget the evil things they have done.'

This seems to be quite a promise, Lord.
And looking around me
   I can't help but wonder
   if it will ever come true.

So many people
   don't believe.
So many people
   haven't a clue about you,
   about what you're about.

This is a world living in ignorance
   of everything that you are.

What can I do about it, Lord?
I'm just one person.
I can't change the world.
I can't open people's minds.
Will this world ever be ready for you, Lord?
Will it ever listen?
Or will it just continue to drift,
   floating further and further
      away from its own loving Creator?

Amen.

We all make promises, but do we keep them? How do you feel if someone breaks a promise to you?

What promises have you made to people? Why did you make them?

What promises has God made to us, his people? How does this affect the way you live your life?

Promises, promises, promises. It's easy not to take them seriously. We all make them, we all break them. So what's another promise other than another way to end up disappointed? Hang on, this is God we're talking about. This isn't a mate down the road who promises to give us back a CD we lent them a week ago! This is our God, our Creator, the one who created us out of love, to live in love, for love! Surely a God-promise is different from a mate-promise? Read the passage again – what do you think? Is this something that was simply said to make people feel better but to not actually be fulfilled? Well, the writers of the New Testament believed that Jesus was the full realisation of Jeremiah's prophecy. It wasn't just a short-term promise, but one with a long-term significance. The arrival of Jesus was the 'new covenant' (which is the meaning of 'New Testament'). Now what do you think about God's promises?

Day 30
Keeping promises

Isaiah 43:15-21

I am the Lord, your holy God, Israel's Creator and King. I am the one who cut a path through the mighty ocean. I sent an army to chase you with chariots and horses; now they lie dead, unable to move. They are like an oil lamp with the flame snuffed out. Forget what happened long ago! Don't think about the past. I am creating something new. There it is! Do you see it? I have put roads in deserts, streams in thirsty lands. Every wild animal honours me, even jackals and owls. I provide water in deserts – streams in thirsty lands for my chosen people. I made them my own nation, so that they would praise me.

OK, Lord,
   I get it now -
   you do keep your promises!
There's no other conclusion, really, is there?
All I have to do
   is have a quick glance through the Bible
   and I see your promises fulfilled everywhere.
It's amazing.

But what does it all mean to me?
These are historical promises.
Promises from a time

and a land
so long ago,
so far away,
that they can't be relevant to me now,
here where I am,
can they?

Or maybe they can.
If you could make promises to those people
so long ago,
and keep them,
perhaps the promises to me,
of eternal life,
a life worth living,
a life with you,
are true after all?

Amen.

God's promises to us mean nothing unless we do some-thing with what we're given. Following God, believing in where he's taking you, isn't just about being saved full stop. It's about putting all that you learn into practice. What is there in your life that shows you're letting God live through you?

You want proof that God keeps his promises? Well, here we get that from Isaiah who reminds us of how God led Moses and his people across the Red Sea. Remember that story? Where Moses commanded the waters to rise up and allow them to walk through? That's what's being referred to here. But something more interesting is said. We're told not to cling to events of the past, not to dwell on what happened a long time ago. Instead we are told to look to the future, to look for something new.

It's easy to waste time thinking about how good things used to be and how perhaps it'll never be the same again. By doing that it's easy to become stale, to wallow in old conquests and glories, instead of looking to tomorrow, taking what we've already learned, being prepared and moving on. It's also easy to wander away from God, but what we need to do is to learn from the past, get ready in the present, and prepare for the future. One which promises to be quite amazing!

Day 31

Passover

John 12:12-13, 19

The next day a large crowd was in Jerusalem for Passover. When they heard that Jesus was coming for the festival, they took palm branches and went out to greet him. They shouted, 'Hooray! God bless the one who comes in the name of the Lord! God bless the King of Israel!' . . .

But the Pharisees said to each other, 'There is nothing that can be done! Everyone in the world is following Jesus.'

It seems odd, Lord.
Here were people
   praising your name as you entered Jerusalem.
They were amazed by you,
   stunned by your actions,
   your miracles,
   your words,
   your whole character.

You, Lord,
   were a person who lit a fire in them.
You made them think,
   they followed you
   and wanted something great to happen.
In you rested so much hope.
What were you thinking that day?

Did you know what would soon happen?
Did you know that as quickly as the crowd would praise you
    they would turn on you?

What scares me, Lord,
    is that like those people that day,
    I wonder if a few days later
    I too would have turned,
    persuaded by the crowd,
    by peer pressure,
    by the wish to not be different.

Forgive me my weaknesses, Lord.

Amen.

How strong are your beliefs? Are you really as sure as you think you are? Or are you swayed by what other people say and do? Do you stay quiet when people say and do things that you know aren't right?

God knows we're weak, that it's not easy to stand up for what we believe, what we think. When was the last time you sat down and seriously asked for a little bit of heavenly help?

Springtime and everyone was congregating in Jerusalem. This was Passover time and people travelled far and wide to be there for the celebrations. This was a feast in remembrance of the nation's liberation from Egypt all those years ago. And here we have Jesus turning up on a donkey (grab a Bible and read the bit I missed out – verses 14-16). This was a direct reference to a biblical prophecy. Want to know which one? Well, just turn back to Zechariah 9:9. Read this bit of the Bible and you can see the changes Jesus was ushering in. This was a humble King, but still triumphant and victorious. And this was a King who would get rid of war chariots and destroy the bows used in battle. This was about ever-conquering love and peace brought about by a humble King. This was Jesus riding on a donkey through Jerusalem at the time of the Passover. The Pharisees were beside themselves. Here was this man, on a lowly donkey, and the people were going crazy! They were meeting him with the branches of palm trees, a symbol of victory. What could they do? Something had to be done to stop everyone following this man . . .

Day 32

Lazarus

John 11:1-4
A man called Lazarus was sick in the village of Bethany. He had two sisters, Mary and Martha. This was the same Mary who later poured perfume on the Lord's head and wiped his feet with her hair. The sisters sent a message to the Lord and told him that his good friend Lazarus was sick. When Jesus heard this, he said, 'His sickness won't end in death. It will bring glory to God and his Son.'

Lord,
   this seems impossible.
I've read through this story a few times
   and it's still hard to believe.
I know you have power,
   but to bring someone back from the grave?
How?
Why?

I guess, Lord,
   that such events seem so strange
   because of where I am in this world.
We don't really believe anything any more.
Everything's so virtual,
   or disposable,
   or computer-generated.

We're obsessed with things that fade
  and are all too happy
  to dismiss those things we don't quite understand.

In this world,
  I find it hard to believe such an event ever took place.
But then I look at the rest of your life,
  what you did with it.
So why should this event be any different?
Why should I doubt that it happened?
Because *if* it did,
  if you raised Lazarus from the grave,
  then I have no choice
  but to listen to you,
  understand your life,
  your actions,
  and what they mean to me.

Help me believe, Lord.

Amen.

What is it in your life that stops you believing in God, in what Jesus did, in what your life could become?

What if these things did happen? What if Jesus did all those things recorded in the New Testament? How does this change the way you look at him, at your own life?

This is a big event. Jesus knows Lazarus will die, but he also knows that he's not about to let death have the last word. He knows his own death lies just round the corner and perhaps as a way of making sure his disciples will believe in him in the coming days, this event takes place. The disciples didn't want him to make the journey to see Lazarus. They were afraid for Jesus' safety. But when Jesus decides to go, Thomas basically says, 'Right, if he's going, then we all go to die with him!' When they arrive, Lazarus has been dead for four days. Martha knows Jesus could have saved Lazarus if he'd arrived in time, but she also believes he can still do something. Mary then meets Jesus and pretty much says the same. Here Jesus sees first hand the effect of death on God's people. The hurt it causes, the fear. But he's going to have the last say and show them death hasn't got a chance. He asks to see Lazarus. At the tomb, Jesus commands Lazarus to come out, and he does: Lazarus is alive – and the people with him knew then that this man had power even over death.

Day 33
Wasted perfume

Mark 14:3-11

Jesus was eating in Bethany at the home of Simon, who once had leprosy, when a woman came in with a very expensive bottle of sweet-smelling perfume. After breaking it open, she poured the perfume on Jesus' head. This made some of the guests angry, and they complained, 'Why such a waste? We could have sold this perfume for more than three hundred silver coins and given the money to the poor!' So they started saying cruel things to the woman.

But Jesus said: 'Leave her alone! Why are you bothering her? She has done a beautiful thing for me. You will always have the poor with you. And whenever you want to, you can give to them. But you won't always have me here with you. She has done all she could by pouring perfume on my body to prepare it for burial. You may be sure that wherever the good news is told all over the world, people will remember what she has done. And they will tell others.'

Sometimes, Lord,
 it's hard to know what to say,
 what words to use.
They don't always come easily.
We're left with no choice
 but to do something,

and actions do so often
seem to speak louder than words.

I wonder if that's what happened here?
Unable to find the words,
   all the woman can do
   is to take her most expensive perfume,
   and pour it on you.
She couldn't find the words
   to say what was in her heart,
   and instead acted them out.

People were annoyed,
   said it was a waste,
   but you knew different.
There was something else here,
   something about preparing you
   for what was to happen soon.
I wonder, Lord,
   if anyone in that room
   really understood your words?

Amen.

Actions speak louder than words. When have you been unable to say what you mean and instead done something to show your feelings?

When people tell you what they think of you, tell you they like you or even love you, it's easy to forget what was said.

But if they do something to demonstrate their feelings, it stays with you, means so much more. It's easy to talk and say what we think, what we believe, but do we put enough of our words into action?

In John 12:3, we read that this woman is actually Mary. The time of Jesus' death is now getting very close. Check out the passages before and after the one you've just read. There are warnings by Jesus of his death. There's the plot by the chief priests and the teachers of the law to arrest Jesus and put him to death. There's the betrayal of Judas, leading to the final meal with the disciples, his arrest and finally death. But in the midst of all this, we have this image of one woman's love for Jesus. In Jesus' time, a little bit of perfume was often poured on to arriving guests as a sign of welcome. It was also used to anoint a body for burial. This is a very symbolic event. Did Mary, more than any other, understand what lay ahead? Perhaps she did. Perhaps she finally began to understand all that Jesus had said, who he was, and she simply couldn't find the words to express her feelings. So she pours the perfume over him, 300 silver coins' worth – a year's wage. Actions do, sometimes, speak louder than words.

Day 34
The last supper

Mark 14:22-26

During the meal, Jesus took some bread in his hands. He blessed the bread and broke it. Then he gave it to his disciples and said, 'Take this. It is my body.'

Jesus picked up a cup of wine and gave thanks to God. He gave it to his disciples, and said, 'Drink it!' So they all drank some. Then he said, 'This is my blood, which is poured out for many people, and with it God makes his agreement. From now on I will not drink any wine, until I drink new wine in God's kingdom.' Then they sang a hymn and went out to the Mount of Olives.

Death scares me, Lord,
and here you are knowing you are soon to face it
and you're sitting with your friends,
trying to get them to realise
all that's going on,
what it all means.

What was that like?
What were you feeling?
What was going on in your head?
Did it all make sense
or was some of it impossible to understand?

Being afraid of death is one thing, Lord,
   but knowing it's just round the corner,
   how it will happen,
   that's something else.
Something you dealt with,
   faced head on
   and then turned on its head.

Help me understand, Lord.

Amen.

What do you think was going on in the minds of the disciples as they heard Jesus speak about the food they were eating as though it was his body? If you had been there, do you think you would have understood any more than they did?

Passover is the celebration of the escape from Egypt, when the blood of lambs was painted above the doors of the houses of the children of Israel, so that the Angel of Death would pass them by. Here Jesus uses this celebration to bring about something new. A lamb was sacrificed to save the people from death all those years ago. Now Jesus takes the place of the Lamb, so that everyone in God's creation would not have to fear death again. In John's Gospel, Jesus is often referred to as the Lamb of God. But that's not all that's taking place – this is a very human story. Was Jesus not the Messiah Judas hoped for? Did the lack of action against the Romans by Jesus finally push him to betray him? Did he really know what he was getting into? The disciples share in the meal with Jesus. They are told by him that the bread and the wine are his body and blood. They know the significance of the meal, but do they really see what Jesus is saying to them? That the old covenant between God and Israel was now to be replaced by something new for everyone? That he was the sacrifice?

Day 35

Jesus is arrested

Matthew 26:47-50, 55-56

Jesus was still speaking, when Judas the betrayer came up. He was one of the twelve disciples, and a large mob armed with swords and clubs was with him. They had been sent by the chief priests and the nation's leaders. Judas had told them beforehand, 'Arrest the man I greet with a kiss.'

Judas walked right up to Jesus and said, 'Hello, teacher.' Then Judas kissed him.

Jesus replied, 'My friend, why are you here?' ...

Jesus said to the mob, 'Why do you come with swords and clubs to arrest me like a criminal? Day after day I sat and taught in the temple, and you didn't arrest me. But all this happened, so that what the prophets wrote would come true.' All Jesus' disciples left him and ran away.

What was Judas thinking, Lord?
Why did he get involved?
It's not as though he needed to.
They wanted you arrested,
    and they have found a way.
Judas, it seems, just got in the way.

What were you feeling at that moment, Lord?
A close friend,

a companion for years,
  betraying you to the people who want you dead.

I can't help but feel sorry for Judas.
He wanted from you
  that which you simply couldn't give.
A revolution that would involve more than love in action,
  getting rid of the Romans, freeing Israel.

You gave freedom,
  but not the freedom he understood.
And it's still that freedom you offer now.
A freedom in God, with God,
  for eternity.
A freedom brought about not by the sword,
  but by love.

Real freedom, Lord.

Amen.

Have you ever felt betrayed by someone? What did it feel like? What did you want to say to this person? What did you want to do? What did you actually do?

Jesus has been praying in the Garden of Gethsemane. Luke describes this very vividly, with the sweat of Jesus falling from him like drops of blood (Luke 22:44). Check out Matthew 26:31-35, and you'll see Jesus preparing the disciples for what is about to happen. They all follow Peter and say that they will die with him. So, the praying is over, Jesus has accepted what he has to do, and then a gang of armed men turn up to take him away. One of Jesus' disciples (in John 18:10, we read that this is Peter) draws his own sword and cuts off the ear from one of those come to arrest Jesus. And Jesus can't believe that after all he has said, they still resort to violence, treating him like a common criminal. He heals the ear of the man (Luke 22:51) and goes with them, and just like he said, his disciples desert him. Everything, it seems, is coming true. His mission is coming to its violent and earth-shattering climax. And Jesus' life, the life of a carpenter from a nowhere town somewhere in history, is about to send shock waves through time.

Day 36
Peter denies Jesus

Luke 22:54-62

Jesus was arrested and led away to the house of the high priest, while Peter followed at a distance. Some people built a fire in the middle of the courtyard and were sitting around it. Peter sat there with them, and a servant girl saw him. Then after she had looked at him carefully, she said, 'This man was with Jesus!'

Peter said, 'Woman, I don't even know that man!'

A little later someone else saw Peter and said, 'You are one of them!'

'No, I'm not!' Peter replied.

About an hour later another man insisted, 'This man must have been with Jesus. They both come from Galilee.'

Peter replied, 'I don't know what you are talking about!' At once, while Peter was still talking, a cock crowed.

The Lord turned and looked at Peter. And Peter remembered that the Lord had said, 'Before a cock crows tomorrow morning, you will say three times that you don't know me.'

Then Peter went out and cried hard.

Lord,
    I deny that I know you
    each and every day of my life:

through the things I say,
the things I do,
the things I think.

I ignore you,
    I walk away from you,
    I hide from you.
And sometimes I even think
    that you don't notice.

Sometimes, Lord,
    I do this because I'm weak,
    because I don't want to be made fun of,
    laughed at.
Other times I do it
    because I'm scared.
And then occasionally I do it
    because I'm just not thinking.

I don't mean to be so weak,
    and even when I do make mistakes,
    I accept them
    and ask for your help.

Which is why I pray, Lord,
    that even when I ignore you,
    you won't ignore me.

Amen.

Put yourself in Peter's shoes. How do you think he felt at that moment? How do you think you would have reacted if you had been in the same position?

How do you think Jesus felt? Remember that he'd already told Peter what he'd do.

First of all, before dwelling on the fact that Peter denied knowing Jesus three times, think about why Peter followed. He's just watched his best friend and teacher being led away by an armed gang. His other friends have bolted and he knows now that one of them betrayed Jesus. But instead of running as well, he plucks up enough courage to follow Jesus. What was going on in his head? Was he secretly wondering if he could do something? That God would give him the strength to overcome the gang surrounding Jesus and save him, take him away? Who knows, but there's no doubt that Peter must have been in total confusion at that moment. And then he has to wait. He's followed Jesus, and he's left suddenly alone with strangers. No friends are with him, it's just him and the questions of the people around the fire. Peter is Jesus' leading disciple, the one he wants to build his Church on, but in this moment, he fails. In the face of the opposition, he weakens and denies ever having known Jesus. And when the cock crows and Jesus reappears and looks at him, he breaks down and weeps. But remember this – Peter is not only Jesus' chosen disciple, he is also so wonderfully human. His emotions are raw and easily exposed.

He says what he thinks, he acts from the heart, and he has his failings. But perhaps it's because of all this that he is chosen by Jesus as the rock of his Church?

Day 37
King of the Jews

Matthew 27:11-13

Jesus was brought before Pilate the governor, who asked him, 'Are you the king of the Jews?'

'Those are your words!' Jesus answered. And when the chief priests and leaders brought their charges against him, he did not say a thing.

Pilate asked him, 'Don't you hear what crimes they say you have done?' But Jesus did not say anything, and the governor was greatly amazed.

You could have changed it all, Lord.
Right there,
   in that moment,
   you could have turned and said who you were,
   proved it,
   given them no cause for doubt.
The world would have shuddered,
   as its servant King stood unveiled on its soil.
People would've had no choice but to believe,
   to understand,
   to follow.
That would've been it.
End of story,
   the beginning of a new order.

But you didn't.
You stood in front of your accusers,
   and were soon on your way
   to your death on the cross.

Did you want to turn to the crowds
   and prove who you were?
Did you want to show them,
   force them to believe?
What stopped you?

Help me to understand your story, Lord,
   and your silence.

Amen.

Why do you think Jesus decided not to prove to the world once and for all exactly who he was?

How do you think people would have reacted if Jesus had shown them his power? Do you really think they would've believed? And if so, would it simply have been out of fear, rather than out of love and faith, as Jesus wanted?

Under Jewish law, blasphemy was a capital charge, a death sentence. This is what the Pharisees wanted Jesus charged with. If he claimed to be the Son of God then that was it, his time was up, and their problem was solved.

Jesus would be killed and they could go back to not having to worry about losing control of the people. But here, in front of Pilate, the charge is instead about claiming to be king of the Jews. Pilate isn't interested in offences against Jewish religious law. He's only interested in keeping the peace, and if Jesus is claiming to be king of the Jews, then this is treason. Someone rising against Herod, claiming to be king, with the people behind him, could lead to huge civil unrest. This is not what Pilate wants, and he certainly doesn't want a bad report on the way he's running things to end up in the hands of the emperor. So what can he do? This is an innocent man in front of him, but he also knows that this innocent man could light a fire that would burn his control of the region to the ground.

Day 38
Sentenced to death

Mark 15:6-15

During Passover, Pilate always freed one prisoner chosen by the people. And at that time there was a prisoner named Barabbas. He and some others had been arrested for murder during a riot. The crowd now came and asked Pilate to set a prisoner free, just as he usually did.

Pilate asked them, 'Do you want me to free the king of the Jews?' Pilate knew that the chief priests had brought Jesus to him because they were jealous.

But the chief priests told the crowd to ask Pilate to free Barabbas.

Then Pilate asked the crowd, 'What do you want me to do with this man you say is the king of the Jews?'

They yelled, 'Nail him to a cross!'

Pilate asked, 'But what crime has he done?'

'Nail him to a cross!' they yelled even louder.

Pilate wanted to please the crowd. So he set Barabbas free. Then he ordered his soldiers to beat Jesus with a whip and nail him to a cross.

I've thought it over in my mind so many times, Lord;
    that moment when you heard the crowds
    demand your death,
    chanting it at you.
The very same crowd who had welcomed you to Jerusalem.

What went wrong?
Why the change?

You were standing next to a known criminal,
    someone everyone knew had done wrong.
He was a terrorist,
    someone who had used violence
    to try to topple the Romans.
You?
You'd used love,
    spoken of love,
    demonstrated love.

It was you they sentenced, you they wanted dead.
The power of love, it seemed in that moment,
    wasn't as powerful
    as a sword or a dagger.

And then you were led away,
    whipped and beaten,
    and finally led to the cross.
Sometimes, Lord,
    none of this makes sense.
Help me understand.

Amen.

Put yourself there, in that crowd. All around you, the
people have turned on Jesus. Whipped up into hatred,
they chant for crucifixion. After all, at what point was this
man, this carpenter, ever going to lead them against the

Romans? He was a charlatan, a liar, a fool. How mad they must have been to believe in him! Better to crucify him and instead have Barabbas, someone who really did something about what he thought, put his thoughts into actions, by the sword. How do you feel? What do you do?

Under Roman rule the Sanhedrin could not carry out the death sentence. They had certain powers, but not all, and by keeping it like this, the Romans had ultimate power and control. And the Romans weren't interested in blasphemy. Treason though was a different matter. If they could convince the Romans that Jesus was guilty of treason, then everything would be OK. But Pilate knew the only reason that Jesus was before him was because the chief priests were jealous. Here was this nobody and he was more popular than they would ever be. Pilate really wouldn't have liked being used by them to get their own way. So to maintain control, and in many ways pass the buck back on to the priests, he relies on something he does at the Passover festival – lets the crowd set one prisoner free. And then the crowd chant for Jesus to be crucified. In Matthew 27:24, we read that Pilate washed his hands in a bowl of water in front of the crowd, saying, 'I am not responsible for the death of this man! This is your doing!' He was washing his hands of the whole event, passing the responsibility on to the priests. They chose to free a known criminal and kill an innocent man. This was down to them.

Day 39
Crucified

Matthew 27:35-40

The soldiers nailed Jesus to a cross and gambled to see who would get his clothes. Then they sat down to guard him. Above his head they put a sign that told why he was nailed there. It read, 'This is Jesus, the King of the Jews'. The soldiers also nailed two criminals on crosses, one to the right of Jesus and the other to his left. People who passed by said terrible things about Jesus. They shook their heads and shouted, 'So you're the one who claimed you could tear down the temple and build it again in three days! If you are God's Son, save yourself and come down from the cross!'

I have no words about this, Lord.
The image in my mind
    of you nailed to some wood,
    dying,
    burns me.
The pain,
    the humiliation.

People throwing insults at you,
    your friends looking at you,
    their world shattered.

It's a scene of total and utter despair.
Everything you'd said,
   everything you'd done,
   nailed to death,
   hung out for all to see.

And then you died, Lord.
You died.

Amen.

How would you have reacted if you'd been one of the disciples watching Jesus nailed to a piece of wood and then left to die? Think about the pain, the confusion, the fear, the sense of hopelessness. Now think that those same people took Jesus' teaching and spread it throughout the world. Those people who saw their teacher shattered on a hill side, were the same people who told everyone about Jesus. Many of them even suffered torture and death. So did this death end everything, or start something?

The cross is a hideous death. It was used by the Romans as a warning. Those sentenced to death were nailed to a cross and then left to die and to rot as a warning to others. This wasn't just a way to get rid of someone, but a way to say to others, 'Step out of line, and we'll do this to you, too.' And that's what happened to Jesus. He was hung up and nailed to wood to die. Death took up to two days. The person crucified would experience excruciating pain from the nails, from hanging there. There would be nowhere to rest. Stretched as they were they'd start to suffocate. The only way to stop this was to stand on your feet, feet nailed to the wood you were hanging on. If prisoners took too long to die, Roman soldiers would often break their legs so that they couldn't hold themselves up any more. And to make sure that they really were dead, they'd stab them in their side with a spear. This was a carefully thought out and particularly hideous death and one the chief priests decided Jesus should have. Easy to believe this was the end of it all, isn't it?

Day 40
The temple curtain

Luke 23:44-46
Around midday the sky turned dark and stayed that way until the middle of the afternoon. The sun stopped shining, and the curtain in the temple split down the middle. Jesus shouted, 'Father, I put myself in your hands!' Then he died.

Lord,
    after three years of ministry,
    you died on a tree,
    on a hill,
    in front of the people you'd tried to help.

Everything you'd said,
    everything you'd done,
    was nailed to a tree
    as a warning to others.

They hoped that your words
    would die with you.
That once you were buried
    so would be your teaching.
You'd be forgotten,
    and everything about you
    would fade to dust.

They were wrong, Lord.
The unthinkable happened,
   the impossible happened.
Three days later,
   three days after the first nail
   split the bones in your wrists,
   you turned the world
   and its values
   and its fears
   on its head.

Do the same to me, Lord.
Resurrect me.

Amen.

Jesus died on a cross, but the story doesn't end there. If it did, you wouldn't be thinking about it now. You wouldn't be reading bits from the New Testament. You wouldn't be thinking about the words Jesus said, what he did. It would've all been forgotten. But it wasn't. And here you are thinking about Jesus death. The question is, though, what are you thinking?

The curtain splitting in the temple is very symbolic. In the temple, the curtain divided the sanctuary from the rest of the temple. Only once a year would the high priest pass through this curtain to meet with God on behalf of the people. This is how they believed they could communicate with God. But now the curtain is torn in two. The barrier is gone and there's no longer any need for someone to intercede. Everyone now has access to God. The final, ultimate sacrifice has been made by Jesus. But it doesn't end there. This is Easter, a time where we don't simply meditate on the death of Jesus, but what happened after, what the disciples saw, what they witnessed and heard and experienced and went on to do. So ask yourself this - if Jesus did die and was never seen again by his disciples, would they have spread the news about him, his life, his teaching? They'd witnessed his brutal death. Everything was over and they were probably frightened for their own lives. Are these the kind of people who would then risk everything for something they'd made up? Would they die for it? Or did something extraordinary happen? In those few days of utter despair, were they suddenly witness to something so amazing, so life-changing, that they couldn't do anything but turn round to the world, face the opposition, and shout out about what happened and what it meant? What do you think?

By the same author

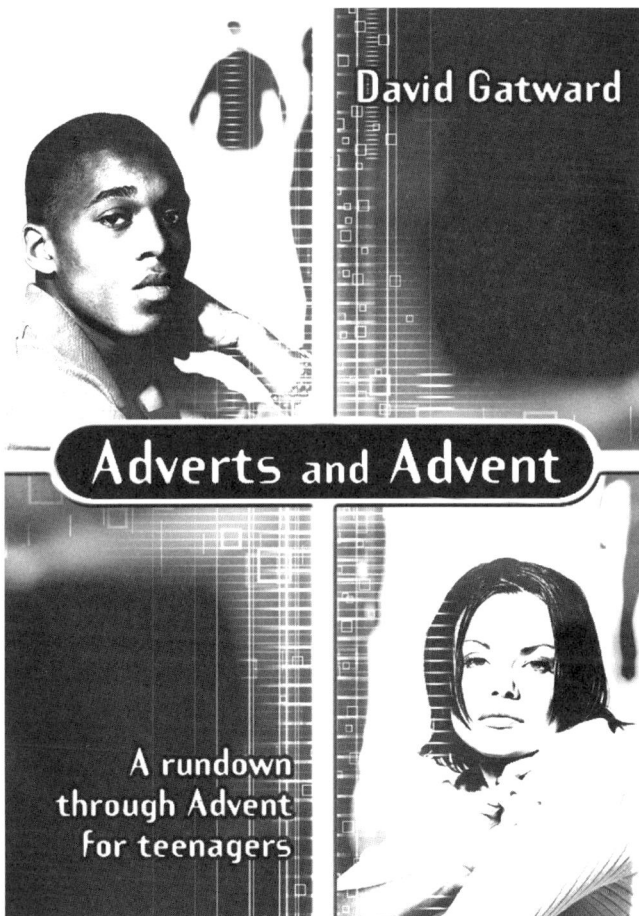

David Gatward

Adverts and Advent

A rundown through Advent for teenagers

ISBN 1 84003 955 8
Catalogue No. 1500538